PRAISE FOR *SURVIVAL:*
'The depth and breadth of this truly imaginative and inspiring body of work reflects the different sectors of society and many regions and countries that have found their way to the University Centre Grimsby to compete in the Hammond House International Poetry Prize.'

Christopher Sanderson

'An imaginative and thoughtful collection of world poetry reflecting a variety of cultures, styles and tastes, but always resonating with the universal truths that affect us all.'

Steve Jackson

'This superb anthology gathers some of the best in modern writing from around the world.'

Hugh Riches, Journalist and Broadcaster

OTHER PUBLICATIONS:

Tales From The Walled Garden

Precious
Award Winning Short Stories

Precious
Award Winning Poetry

Shakespeare In Debt
by Ted Stanley

Who's Afraid Of The Dark – Not Me!
by Sarah Smith

Cows In Trees
by Julian Earl

The Dog With The Head Transplant
by Julian Earl

25 Years On: Grimsby Writers
Short Stories and Poems

Leaving
Award Winning Short Stories

Leaving
Award Winning Poetry

Survival
Award Winning Short Stories

SURVIVAL
AWARD WINNING POETRY
Edited by Ted Stanley

SURVIVAL
AWARD WINNING POETRY

1st Edition published in the UK in 2021 by
Hammond House Publishing Ltd

ISBN: 978-1-91-609808-4

The right of the individual writers to be identified as the author of this work has been asserted in accordance with sections 77 and 78 of the Copyright Designs and Patents act 1988.

All rights reserved. No part of this publication may be reproduced, stored in a retrieval system, or transmitted in any form or by any means, electronic, mechanical, photocopying, recording or otherwise, without the permission of the Publisher in writing.

Page Design by Alex Thompson
Proofreading by Jennie Liebenberg
Cover Design by Ted Stanley

Cover Image *SURVIVAL* by Deborah Geddes, first exhibited in 2020. Produced by permission of the artist.
All rights reserved.

The opinions expressed in this book are entirely those of the individual authors and are not endorsed or supported by the publishers or their sponsor, University Centre Grimsby.

Contains language that may be considered unsuitable for a younger audience.

Hammond House Publishing Ltd
13 Dudley Street, Lincolnshire
DN31 2AE, United Kingdom

www.hammondhousepublishing.com

SURVIVAL
AWARD WINNING POETRY

Enjoy this eclectic collection of poetry that brings together award winning writers from around the world.

SURVIVAL is the fifth in a series of poetry anthologies, each featuring a different theme and including the winning and shortlisted stories from the annual *Hammond House International Literary Prize*.

Includes the winner of the
2020 International Literary Prize

The opinions expressed in this book are entirely those of the individual authors and are not endorsed or supported by the University Centre Grimsby.

Contents

Introduction | *Ted Stanley*	xii
The Inheritence | *Donald Adamson*	2
Come back to me | *Keira Brite*	5
Little Water Bear | *Jane Burn*	6
The Soldier's Sandals | *Francesco Capussela*	8
Walkabout | *Jean Cooper Moran*	10
ABSALOM. | *John Coughlan*	12
As Found | *Eloise Curtis*	14
La Moselle | *Karina Fiorini*	16
A Call To Arms | *Ruth Flanagan*	18
On The Wings of an Albatross | *Ruth Flanagan*	20
The great silence | *Will Hatchett*	22
Climatic | *Dick Heath*	24
Bring My Daddy Home | *Marcus Jones*	26
For the 'anti-racists' who believed one black square was enough | *Tiffany King*	28
Survival | *Meg Macleod*	34
Florescence | *Meredith Mars*	36
Perhaps we'll die | *Bruce Marsland*	40
Two Bites! | *Donald McCrory*	42

Contents

Dirt | *Mason Nunemaker*	44
The Night Nurse | *Fadekemi Olumide-Aluko*	46
Island of the Living Dead | *Val Ormrod*	48
The Picnic | *John Plowright*	50
Survival | *Abi G Richardson*	52
Labelled | *Noeleen Smullen*	54
Sunday Papers | *Ted Stanley*	56
Back to the Sea | *Anne Steward*	58
Remembrance Day | *Tim Taylor*	60
West Shore | *Tim Taylor*	62
More than alive; | *Dawn Vincent*	64
Birthday Cake | *Matthew Wixey*	66
Choices | *Valerie Wynne*	68
Survival, But | *Kathy Zwick*	70

Illustrations

Glynne Bulman	2
Glynne Bulman	5
Rachel Sené	6
Glynne Bulman	8
Glynne Bulman	10
Glynne Bulman	12
Margaret Inkpen	14
Glynne Bulman	16
Glynne Bulman	18
Glynne Bulman	20
Doriano Solinas	22
Joanne Maltby	24
Margaret Inkpen	26
Glynne Bulman	28
Glynne Bulman	34
Joanne Maltby	36
Sarah Palmer	40
Glynne Bulman	42

Illustrations

Doriano Solinas	44
Glynne Bulman	46
Glynne Bulman	48
Joanne Maltby	50
Rachel Sené	52
Rachel Sené	54
Doriano Solinas	56
Meg Macleod	58
Joanne Maltby	60
Meg Macleod	62
Doriano Solinas	64
Doriano Solinas	66
Margaret Inkpen	68
Sarah Palmer	70

Acknowledgments

Alex Thompson, Deborah Geddes, Jennie Liebenberg, Leanne Doyle, Jonathon and Katherine Williams-Stanley and Richard Hall.

The University Centre Grimsby for sponsoring the International Literary Prize and the National Lottery Community fund for supporting our writer's groups. Competition Judges: William Hatchett, Steve Jackson and Paul Sutherland.

The artists whose beautiful illustrations accompany the poems: Glynne Bulman, Rachel Sené, Margaret Inkpen, Doriano Solinas, Joanne Maltby, Sarah Palmer and Meg Macleod.

Finally, all the writers who submitted such a wonderful collection of poems. We are sorry we were unable to include more.

Introduction

OUR PROPHETIC THEME for the 2020 International Literary Prize inspired a record number of wonderful poems, challenging the judges like never before. All the shortlisted entries are here for you to enjoy and judge for yourself.

Until the onset of the Coronavirus pandemic, the struggle for survival often seemed remote when viewed through the lens of supposedly civilised societies: the famine-stricken people of Yem- en, the favelados of Brazil, or endangered species across the planet. However, 2020 saw the struggle for survival touch all of our lives.

The writers in this anthology explore what it means to survive in this increasingly volatile world. From the Coronavirus pandemic, and the plight of people in war-torn countries across the world, to the political upheaval that characterised this tumultuous year, the poems in this anthology reflect the different ways in which people have survived.

Also included are poems from the competition judges and my choices of international entries from countries where the first language isn't English, reflecting the geographical and cultural diversity of Hammond House members and competition entrants.

Survival is a collaborative effort, representing the mission of Hammond House to support talented people and encourage collaboration between all the creative arts. Each poem in this anthology is accompanied by a beautiful illustration from one of seven talented artists, who were tasked with bringing the words of the writers to life, adding a new dimension to this fascinating collection of poetry from around the world

We are delighted, proud and privileged to be publishing this outstanding body of work.

TED STANLEY

'Friendship is unnecessary, like philosophy, like art…
It has no survival value; rather it is one of those things
that give value to survival.'

C.S Lewis

Editor's Choice

The Inheritance
Donald Adamson
Finland

John A – my forebear,
name-giver, border-crosser
and promise-breaker who abandoned
my great-great-grandmother
and the bastard bairn he gave her –

a fellow of craft it seems
more than virtue. In the records he's
a millwright. What is it about mills
and wanderlust? – I'll have that
and a few other odds and ends

worth keeping: thrumming wheel-music,
metre in the slap-slap-slap of paddles,
rhythmic and percussive, down and up,
passion in the gush and leap
of water from the millrace. And maybe

satisfaction of a job well done
and a last look-back
to comprehend every part working
as it should. With money sitting snug
and proudly in his pocket. Moving on.

Editor's Choice

Come back to me
Keira Brite
Netherlands

You bleed blue, I know you do.
Do you think they know too?
Do you know how often it's you, only you?
Your strength that gets me through?
And it breaks my heart to see these two
try everything they can to break you!
But I know you. I know you.
And the hero is no hero if not proved.
Fight your demon. Slay your dragons.
Recover that power that was taken from you.
Let it strengthen your heart.
Then come back to me 'you'.

SHORTLISTED ENTRY

Little Water Bear
Jane Burn
United Kingdom

Tiny, titchy, totty, tiddler of a thing –
I am smaller that you thought a bear could be.
Here in my miniature land of mossy trees, I place

my little feet, claws spun like invisible thread,
legs like bitsy dumpling rolls, body a bead
of eensy-weensy dough. Sometimes I curl

my tincey plump into a tun and waste myself dry
through a hundred bitty years of cryptobiotic sleep.
I have been to boiling point, have frozen

my plump-self stiff yet I seem to be un-killable, indestructible.
Just add water and watch my withered, dinky life go ping!
They sent me to outer space and I lived, lips pursed

in their permanent, pin-head O. I am a safe-from-the Arctic,
deep-sea, desert, absolute zero cutesy, squishy dot of a pig and
I was here before dinosaurs – asteroids have struck and I have
plodded on,

too light to leave a footprint. I have travelled slowly, taken time
to place each of my tardy steps through litters of fallen leaves.
I do not need to eat (if food be short) for up to thirty years

and so there is no greed, no landfill spoil from me –
just meals of lichen, pure and green. My kind will live
until the sun burns out and then, perhaps long after.

The apocalypse might come but we will slumber through
the worst, wake when rain falls fresh again upon the scalded earth.
I will keep my steady progress, float like a bantam-weight balloon

and think of how you never really knew that I was there,
paddling beneath the crushing of your giant feet. We might grieve
but you would never see our microscopic tears.

NOTES

Tardigrades (also known as water bears or moss piglets) are
micro-creatures who measure up to 1.5mm. They live in water,
lichen and mosses and have been widely studied for their ability
to survive for years in extreme conditions. Scientists predict that
they will be the last creature to survive the end of the world.

HIGHLY COMMENDED

The Soldier's Sandals
Francesco Capussela
United States

The homeless lieutenant wears
Ancient memories of violence
Staring at his leather sandals.

The sand his timeshare,
The shore his muddy neighbors.
He catches some ocean
In his rusty helmet
Preparing for war.

The vagabond soldier
Fills his pockets
With the empty city.
Civilians have been vacuumed
By the morning street sweeper.

As an eagle upon the cement river
A newspaper fiercely flies on the avenue
Finding a nest between the free man's feet.

A corner smells of ink.
Friday, May 29, 2020.
He makes a birthday wish
Visiting the unfriendly asphalt.

A protester platoon
Materializes from the
Silent cinema corner.
The war movie in his head
Plays its final tune
As the credits roll
With bitter reality.

Society finally gave a gift
To the black visage
Reflected in the darker void
Of the shoe shop window.

Time to take the sandals off.

First Place

Walkabout
Jean Cooper Moran
United Kingdom

My mother gave birth on the red road as I wriggled my way through her long journey
I kicked and squirmed in her soft red cradle
drawing the salty liquid in with ease, expelling the same
I was unapologetically unrefined, raw, of no value
except to the woman who carried me crooning constantly
stroking me with love and no regrets even at the times of greatest pain
her hypnotising lalala wound into my watery crib
sparing shocks as she walked to her goal
she sought rest and helping hands to make her well again
I sought release, uncompromising in my intention. I spared her nothing
at times she rested, all the many reverberations stilled in my world
we were at peace together she and I
and when she breathed, she pulled the sharp atoms of dry landscape into her chest
I waited floating in warm oblivion, all movement slowed until she woke frantic for food
crouching in the bushes retching, snared by her body wastes
she vibrated to her hunger, walking without pause
I heard rough music, shrill squeals from her empty gut and hollow spaces

stumbling from side to side suddenly without thought for I, myself always feeding from her fading strength.
as the day's heat mounted, degree on degree making a cauldron of her lungs she stopped again, leaned down and vomited
the shocks thrummed in my world of warm repose, waking me, making me kick
I pounded her cradle in rage as she fell to her knees, caught by kind hands
calling for help and clutching her stomach
I felt them pressing on my limbs giving us reassurance that I lived
then I rested, stretching my body to the limit then curling once again
her heartbeat sounding through my water world and the blood rush hissing in my ears

Shortlisted Entry

ABSALOM.
John Coughlan
United Kingdom

(For my son John Denis, already a better man than I)

What is this huge thing
I feel for you my Son?
The cry of David
Swells on the tides of the moon
And breaks upon the bitter beaches
Of my stricken soul.
I am more afraid than you
That here you lie again
My hands twisting over
My gaunt and wasted kindling boy
Draped in wringing sheets.
Your hair, caught in a thicket web
Of bed, and beeps, and tubes.
Lit by flickering screens you seem
An alien, regenerating all his strength
Amid the electronic chatter of his alcove.
The depth of the wee hours has brought
Jack the Pumpkin King to mind,
My head down low across your
Brittle stick thin arm where
My tears have made you stir.
I feel your hand a gentle balm,
Soft benediction on my head

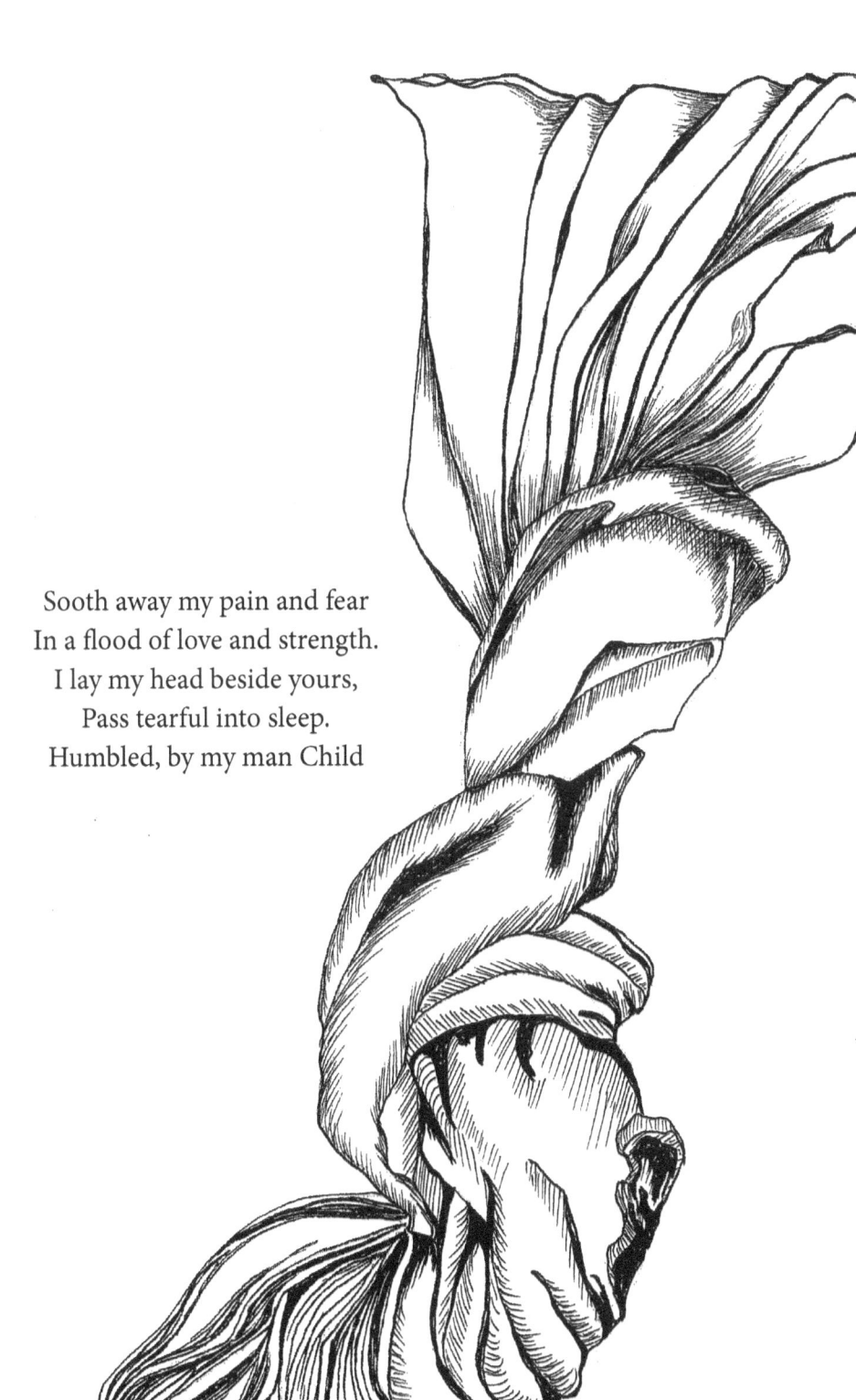

Sooth away my pain and fear
In a flood of love and strength.
I lay my head beside yours,
Pass tearful into sleep.
Humbled, by my man Child

SHORTLISTED ENTRY

As Found
Eloise Curtis
United Kingdom

Strings hold her together
A threadbare doll
Tatty, worn and unsaleable

Garish blue thread
Expertly knotted
Prevent her insides from falling out.

She isn't all that old
The years have been unkind
With better care
She could've been pristine

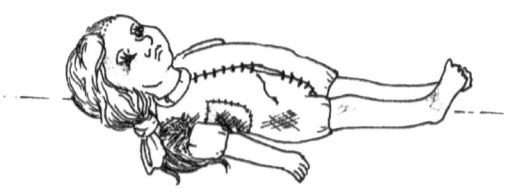

Instead
Other dolls
Dolls with no scrapes or patches or grubby marks
Change clothes with summery smiles.

The latest short short dress
Dangling earrings
Soft feet into hard heels.
Expressions never changing

This doll hides her body
Hides the 'accidents', the rough play
And the tears to her outer fabric.

Gathering dust on the highest shelf
She sits in the corner
Mute
Her glass eyes shimmer
For her words have fallen one too many times
On deaf ears.

Editor's Choice

La Moselle
Karina Fiorini
Luxembourg

To while away time
we hide in between Champagne
and the Vosges,
drink some Moselle, eat a little *pâte sucrée*
lip the wild berries blue, miss the TGV
sleep under the bower
of memories at Lunéville Château, *quelle vue*!

To while away time
we snack on oat bran ne'ar
the stream blue,
rectangle clouds pillowed bulbs
blush the morning nectar, limn the bedrock
as the rills meander, we lay near a five star ant hotel,
it happens this way

To while away time
we hear mass at *Saint Étienne's*
like two tramps,
catch *les dernières nouvelles*, in
the mirabelle liquor our lips
a golden madeleine, we're flammable
like old celluloid films, it happens this way

We breath in the esplanade, *sans limites*
the tannic sun wends our skin,
from the new temple, round ramparts
field notes in *Rue Taison*

Le Graoully en garde, streetscapes shift,
arms morphe, his pulse on my loin.

Shortlisted

A Call To Arms
Ruth Flanagan
United Kingdom

I dreamt that I was on top of a mountain
and all I could see was death and dust.
A toxic gas hung in the sky,
stifling the air in a shroud of heat.

"Where am I?" I cried.
"What have we done?" But no one replied.

As I climbed lower, hot stones blistered my feet
and Earth lay scorched and bare before me.
Instead of oceans, craters formed
bottomless graveyards of the dead.

"What madness!" I gasped.
"We must act now to right what has passed.

"Come quickly!" I called to the youth left on Earth.
"You have the power to safeguard rebirth.
Reverse the damage caused by man's greed.
Remove the noose and let the world breathe.

Unite!" I wailed.
"You must succeed where others have failed."
Then out of the wasteland, the young people crept.
"Take courage," I yelled. "Let your voices be heard.
From your anguish raise an army.
Bring the dead back to the living.

You are the future," I cried.
"If you give in, who else will try?"

So they smashed up the engines that poisoned the air
and stood triumphant hand in hand.
Where their tears fell, rivers flowed
and shoots of green burst through the dust.

"We are the guardians of life," they cheered,
"that share the Earth with all things dear."

Then forests grew up where the land was laid bare
and creatures came and reared life anew.
Where the shroud had covered the sky,
birds swooped and soared in realms of blue.

"Together we are strong," they said.
"Life thrives again where once it was dead."

Judge's Choice

On The Wings of an Albatross
Ruth Flanagan
United Kingdom

Oh Albatross that boldly flies
Across the vast, perpetual skies,
Let me fly upon your wings
And see the wonders shared by kings.
For you have flown beside the sun
And watched it set when day is done,
Then gazed as colours paint the sky
And ripple through the clouds on high.

Wanderer of endless seas
That rise and fall eternally,
Let me glide across the blue
And fly the way of dreams with you.
For you have seen the dawn's first rays
Burst forth like gold dust on the waves,
And through ethereal skies have flown
To watch the world from Heaven's throne.

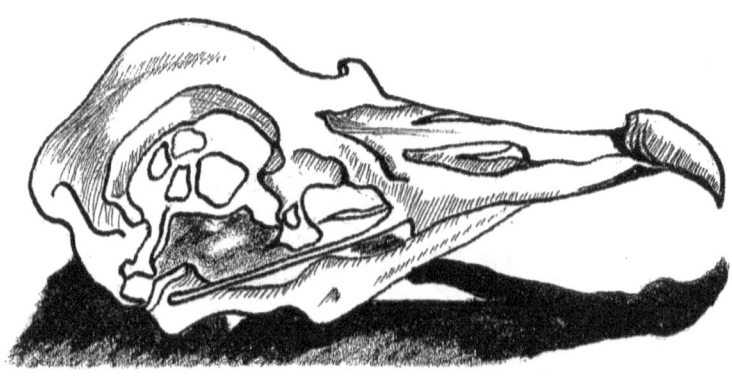

Intrepid bird of land and sky,
That knows the Earth far more than I,
Take me with you please, I pray,
Far from these urban sprawls of grey.
Away from where the chimneys rise
And smoke and grime pollute the skies,
To where in dreams I can be free
And see how things were meant to be.

Oh Albatross that bravely roams
And guides the weary traveller home,
Show me how to find the way
To reach you at the end of day.
For dreaming helps me to survive
The daily drudgery of life,
And takes me back to far off lands
To fall asleep on sun kissed sands.

The great silence
Will Hatchett
United Kingdom

That year spring came unnoticed.
It whispered to us from outside
in the curious languages of birds
that were normally unheard.

We had moved inside. The skies had emptied
erased of humans and their quaint terrors
as the virus lumbered across the world
in a pestilence of numbers and words.

Inquisitive observers, self-exiled
we watched the planet that we had poisoned
pressed back by the great silence.
We were prisoners locked in glass houses

trapped by an epidemic of loneliness
reading a message that nature did not need us.

Shortlisted

Climatic
Dick Heath
United Kingdom

Today we're all so busy.
No-one's seeing all the signs.
Our poor round world is shouting,
But we're not listening all the time.
Things keep changing all around us,
Today we're flooded out.
The rivers get so swollen.
What's that really all about?
We're simply not seeing
What's just around the bend.
Is there time for us to wake up
Or stand watching it all end?
Can we have a brand new future?
It's well within our powers.
Do we need to make more plastic
To clad all our 'Grenfell Towers'?
We should insulate all our homes
With hemp or soft sheep's wool,

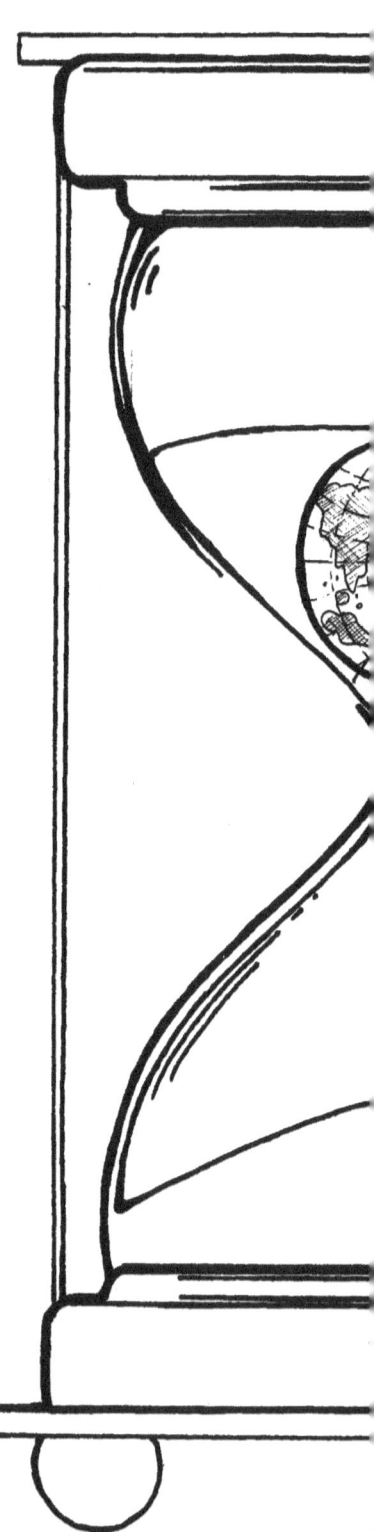

And stop blaming all the cows
That we threaten, now, to cull.
Those polluting cars keep driving:
Our favourite sets of wheels,
Distributing deadly vapours,
Ignoring our children's pleas.
All our bright new tomorrows
Could be captured from the sky,
Or blown through whirling wind farms
With a long, electric sigh.
The technology is with us.
Let's keep our world alive.
Or watch it go completely dead,
Leaving nowhere to survive.
Please, everyone, just listen.
The words are on the breeze.
Our world around begs for our help,
Falling down upon its knees.

SHORTLISTED

Bring My Daddy Home
Marcus Jones
United Kingdom

Near the city of Palmyra, where the silk road once passed through,
lived a community of Muslim, of Christian and of Jew.
They lived in peace and harmony, though poverty as well;
revolution then erupted, turned paradise to hell.

IS fighters stormed the town, to fight the tyranny,
passed guns and threats and mortars, barked orders angrily.
Now neighbours despise neighbours, religion stokes the hate;
beheadings of dissenters, with chants of *God is great!*

Fighter jets are swarming, they're screaming overhead.
They bombed my grand pa's home last night, and grand mama is dead.
The sky's a raging furnace, the horizon's flashing red;
no mercy on either side, just suffering instead

I feel the hairs rise on my neck as I find somewhere to hide;
my heart is bursting out my chest, bullets at every stride.
A bomb explodes just down our street and covers us in mud,
my head was hit by shrapnel; I am crying tears of blood.

I hear the men chant to the Lord, I hear the soldiers run;
the screams of mums and mortars, rat tat of machine guns.
Choppers, dust and bomb blasts; black smoke plumes fill the air;
buildings fall, to screams and chants, and panic everywhere.

The neighbours are all dead now, there's no one here to save;
the army shot and threw them all, in a bottomless mass grave.
Brown tanks rumbled down the street, and blasted our front door;
mum's lying in a pool of blood, limbs splayed across the floor.

My sister lies unconscious, near grandpa's rocking chair;
by her toys and birthday dress, and new shoes she'll never wear.
Hoarse whispers can't awaken them; they appear to be asleep;
The fallen ceiling's trapped my back, and I can't feel my feet.

A crescent moon sets in the sky, the start of another day;
There's a wail from a far off minaret, calling us to pray.
I am only six years old; I feel weak and so alone;
Wherever you are, please stop this war,
    - - - - - - and bring my daddy home.

For the 'anti-racists' who believed one black square was enough

Tiffany King
United Kingdom

You were silent
You heard
You saw
    You chose to do nothing
       Until one day
You

      Posted a single black square
  And I'm trying to work out
If
You thought a simple blackout
On social media
Would blackout the past,
The present,
The truth.

And so
You
Joined the trend
For one day
Maybe even a week.

When it was fashionable to be anti-racist.

When did it become too much for you?
A week of challenging conversations
With family and friends
Who were shocked, surprised,
Saddened
That you shared a black square?

So
You
Effectively rescinded
Your superficial support
With another
Socially and emotionally
Distanced
Swipe, share, like
Of a comment
Fashioned and formed
In retaliation.

Pause.

I repeat.

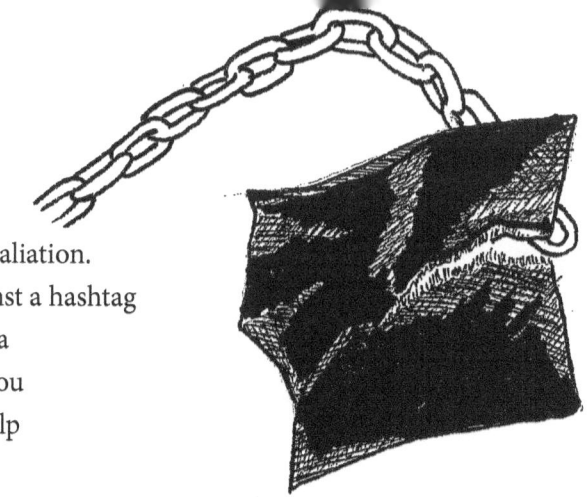

In retaliation.
Against a hashtag
A plea
For you
To help
Me
Us
Dismantle systemic racism
Institutionalised prejudice.
Together.

So that one day
Our children won't need to cry out
Black lives matter.

But maybe you don't share that dream?
For me
For us

How else did you manage to listen
To our pain
And neatly compartmentalise
Centuries of discrimination
And
Reduce it to one incident
In the U.S?

I wonder
If
You are still reading
Or if you switched off
Because I'm writing another post
And I haven't 'got over it yet!'
A legacy of selective amnesia
Which
You
Happily, ignorantly adopt.

I thought you had listened
But
Hidden behind a veneer
Of liberal smiles
Platitudes
Emojis
Was the truth.

You choose
To remain yoked to
racial bias.

You

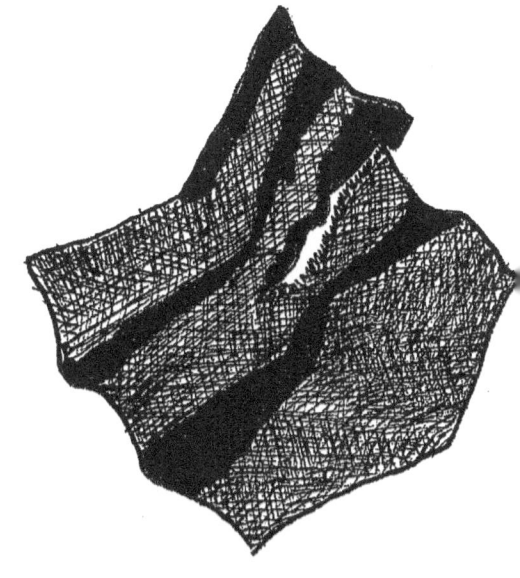

without flinching
try to tell me
to my face
a mixed race British woman
That all black people are homogenous!

What else did you mean?
When you said
'they'
The people you choose to blame
Who only have skin colour in common
'Reflect Me'.

You said this
With concern
You
Smiled sweetly
Not meaning any harm
(Of course not!)
You're not racist.
You have black friends.

How dare you.

Stop hiding behind your cracked veneer.
Racist ideologies
Stereotypes perpetuated
Have no place
Now.

For the sake of our children's future.
…

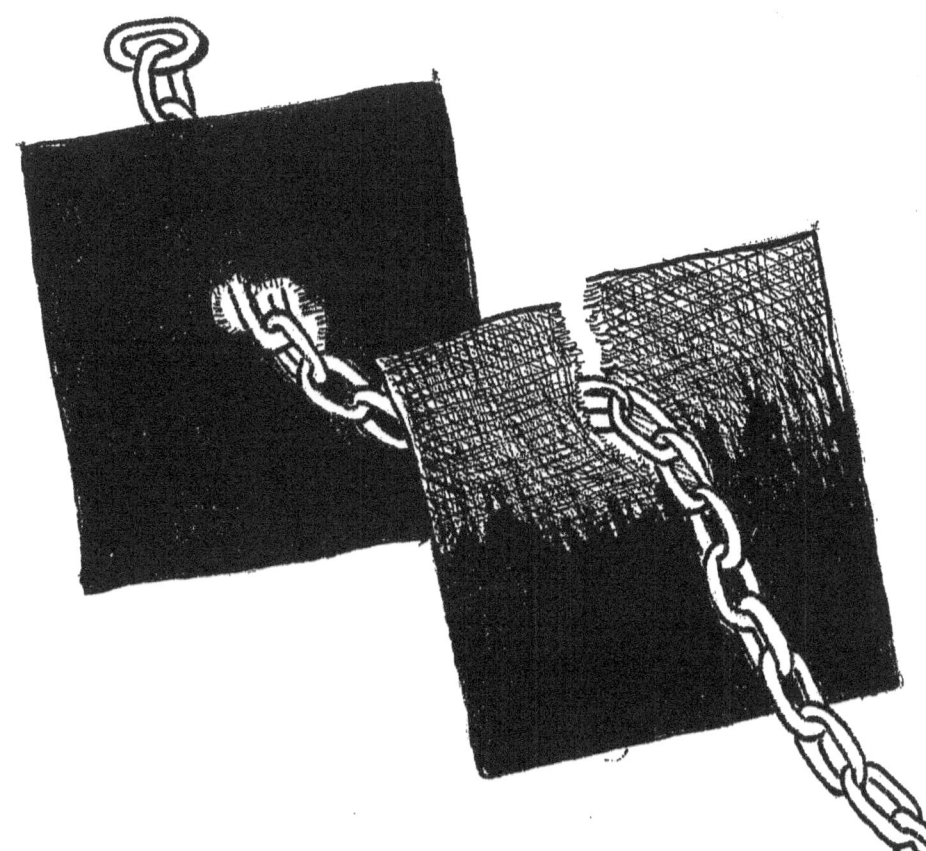

SHORTLISTED

Survival
Meg Macleod
United Kingdom

because love is rare
and appears without definition
she makes excuses
she spends hours painting in the gaps
and over the bruises
sorting through splintered blossoms
of her expectations

into a family friendly jigsaw
she frames the abuse

everything outside the frame fades
sunlight is shaded
music is muted
points of reference clipped
into a perfect thorny thicket
behind which she disappears
her voice a whisper no-one can hear

Shortlisted

Florescence
Meredith Mars
United Kingdom

I am building a home inside myself
from scraps of kindness and splintered peace;
I bind all the things I love about myself
to all the ways I am enough as I am,
to create a shelter strong enough to weather the fiercest of storms:
a calm glade in a concrete jungle.

I am repurposing my flight response,
sanding down old scarred beams of self-neglect and repainting them
in bright dandelion yellow,
softening the sharp edges of expectation into gentle slopes of
acceptance.
I am turning circular thinking into revolutionary thought.
I no longer fit inside the panic room I built as a child
(for although I am not much taller
I have grown so much),
so I turn it into an open display case for all the masks I used to wear;
I hand-write each one's name underneath it
alongside the date I retired it due to lack of demand.

When my mind aches, I run it a bath of soothing sounds
and wrap it in a fluffy towel of kitten videos;
when my soul hungers, I feed it high fantasy and nature documentaries,
washed down with my best friend's laughter;
when sadness visits, I do not deny it—
I greet it as an honoured guest,
cook it a hot meal of acknowledgement and understanding,
and tuck it into bed under sheets knitted from self-compassion.
I exist in full colour, high contrast, and oversaturated hues.
I laugh loudly, and often.
I do not cover my mouth with my hand when I smile.
I do not fold myself down like origami to fit within
hearts too small to contain the whole of me.
I do not kneecap my affections, nor do I censor my hurt.
I do not speak myself smaller,
more palatable,
easier to swallow.
I do not set myself alight to warm frigid hands and cold hearts.

I treat my body not as a graveyard or a temple, but a garden—
I do not try to shame it into submission.
Instead, I tend its borders.
I feed it,
water it,
mostly, I wait through its frequent winters:
I have found that frost thaws faster without being hurried;
not everything beautiful blooms all year round.
I will flower again when I am ready.
I will be ready
soon.

SHORTLISTED

Perhaps we'll die
Bruce Marsland
United States

There was a hot summer that made the grass dry.
We all know why it made the grass dry.
Perhaps we'll die.

There was a hot summer that caused endless fires,
Burning the forests and polluting the air.
It caused endless fires when it made the grass dry.
We all know why it made the grass dry.
Perhaps we'll die.

There was a hot summer that thawed ancient ice
So permafrost oozed and glaciers expired.
It thawed ancient ice when it caused endless fires.
It caused endless fires when it made the grass dry.
We all know why it made the grass dry.
Perhaps we'll die.

There was a hot summer that let methane fly
To mingle with carbon way up in the sky.
It let methane fly when it thawed ancient ice.
It thawed ancient ice when it caused endless fires.
It caused endless fires when it made the grass dry.
We all know why it made the grass dry.
Perhaps we'll die.

There was a hot summer that brewed up a storm
When carbon and methane made the seas warm.
It brewed up a storm when it let methane fly.
It let methane fly when it thawed ancient ice.
It thawed ancient ice when it caused endless fires.
It caused endless fires when it made the grass dry.
We all know why it made the grass dry.
Perhaps we'll die.

There was a hot summer that swelled the high tides,
Which flooded our cities and much more besides.
It swelled the high tides when it brewed up a storm.
It brewed up a storm when it let methane fly.
It let methane fly when it thawed ancient ice.
It thawed ancient ice when it caused endless fires.
It caused endless fires when it made the grass dry.
We all know why it made the grass dry.
Perhaps we'll die.

There was a hot summer that drowned lands far and wide.
Do you think we'll survive?

Judge's Choice

Two Bites!
Donald McCrory
Spain

About to bite an apple after lunch
she looked again at what she hadn't seen:
a full four seasons' ripeness sunset red,
evolving from a seed as old as earth,
swelling in the mid-day sun, maturing
under midnight's melting moon,
full of existential fruitfulness,
alive, and part of everything alive,
enduring nature's constant change of will,
triumphing over birds and toothless worms
and the thieving hands of hungry school-boys,
lingering as they hurry home to tea,
tempted by the sweetness in their eye.

Supported by the tree that gave it life
it looks upon the world we think we know
refusing nothing, ever open like
a flower to heaven's every whim and wish:
scorching suns, raging winds, freezing frosts
as if predestined to be the toy of climate change.
But no! Resistant to the games of the gods
and to the toxic sprays of insecticides
attacks by maggot flies, codling moths, capsid
bugs and to aphids and the dreaded caterpillar

and even worse, the canker of Coronavirus, it thrives
– for apples have learnt to turn the other cheek –
and boldly stand their ground against great odds
as stark reality seeps through their rain-rich skin
stoically awaiting the final sacrifice:
aware that rebirth is guaranteed,
despite deep hungry bites after lunch or
cremation in oven-baked apple pie.

Third Place

Dirt
Mason Nunemaker
United States

One day I met a man with seeds, looking
for any dark place to plant them.

When I opened my mouth to speak, he saw
black in the back of my throat.

He must have mistaken me for dirt.

The roots of his flowers wrapped themselves
around my windpipe. I cannot make a sound.

If you see him,
tell him I am blooming.

I didn't know how to separate
the plant from the body
so I am growing along with it.

Tell him I am not just dirt.
Tell him I am a lush field.
Tell him I am a forest in the making.

Tell him one day I'll grow so tall
he will never see the sun again.

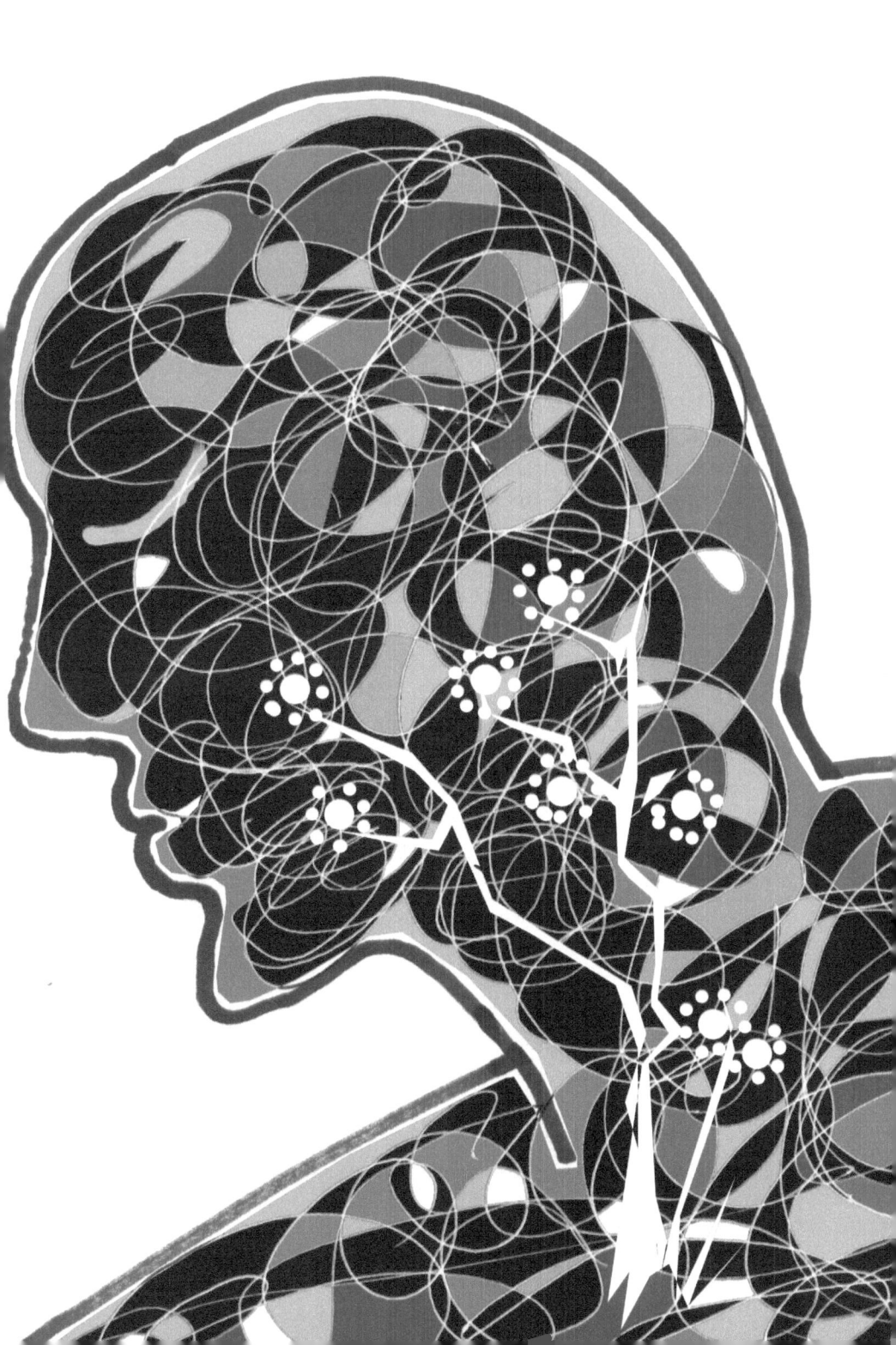

SHORTLISTED

The Night Nurse
FADEKEMI OLUMIDE-ALUKO
Nigeria

Her pot belly always entered my hut first, then the rest of her
She carried it with pride under cheap clothes and bursting waistbands
The kind Papa used to buy at the 'bend-down-select' markets
Before his politics chauffeured us to wildly green pastures

She waddled when she walked
Dragging bowling balls for feet that tortured the slippers covering them
Her gait spoke before she did, "I don't care what you think!"
I cursed the fool who gave her the fat chip on her shoulder

Her cherry-coloured hair made a false claim to youth
Which her all-white undergrowth easily denied
She wore far too much make up
Eye brows painted like fishing hooks
Face full of eye lids and lashes, cheeks and origami lips
All vying for attention from a remarkably blind suitor
"Notice us…we are here…we matter," they said

I hated her the moment I saw her
But I was too perfect then to show it
Conditioned by an education that masked disdain with propriety
And ignorance with Queens English and table manners
So, I mustered a pleasant brand of silence every day
And in exchange, she nursed my burns
Till she judged the chief's daughter ready for her story

She chewed her gum loudly as she talked of her childhood
Of the scheduled defilement she'd endured at her father's hands
And the consuming aloofness of a walking-dead mother
Who enjoyed the numbing therapy of Friday vigils at the local Pentecostal
While her daughter faced a different kind of ritual those holy nights

She recounted how she sought out the familiar, again and again
The last Familiar should have killed her
But she'd stabbed his pulsing neck and refused to die
Now death had lost all patience with her and come to me instead
In a fire lit by my kinsmen to punish my father
I should have been an easier target, surely
But here I was…healing…mattering
Smiling through tears with my brassy night nurse
Two lionesses comparing scars under the African moon

SHORTLISTED

Island of the Living Dead
Val Ormrod
United Kingdom

(Spinalonga, Crete, 1910)

All hope abandon, ye who enter here
                (Dante Alighieri, Inferno)

Dante's words at the gates of Hell
echo here after all these years
with the suffering they foretell.

Like a great warship, the land rears
out of the sea, and the gate looms,
leading to that dark place of fears.

Would they find nothing but tombs
of other lepers gone before?
Would this island spell their own doom?

Shunned as unclean by rule of law,
with just a suitcase, they were led
onto boats to take them ashore

this island of the living dead.
Amid tears, they left old lives behind –
arriving lame and sick with dread.

They found people far from resigned –
the spirit of Spinalonga
was vibrant, with duties assigned.

As doctors helped them live longer,
they loved, married, even gave birth
and the will to survive grew stronger.

There was sadness but also mirth.
Staunch faith gave them new strength to cope.
They valued this world for its worth.

To hell with Dante – they found hope!

SHORTLISTED

The Picnic
JOHN PLOWRIGHT
United Kingdom

Eric and I picnicked
We didn't wander far
But made sure on our journey
To wear the yellow star
And after food and drink
Whilst sitting on the heather
We kissed and dared to think
About our life together
But clouds began to gather
Where to shelter from the storm?
Encircling arms would not suffice
To keep us safe and warm
What lasts? What to hold on to
When war is in the air?
He held me ever closer
And stroked my auburn hair
Then he produced his camera
And captured me on film
Smiling like a blushing bride
Before her dashing groom
That picture Eric took of me
I passed on to a friend
I can't remember why now
I must have known the end
Unspoken premonition
I'd never be his wife
So planted proof like seeds to show
I'd once known love and life

SHORTLISTED

Survival
Abi G Richardson
United Kingdom

At first, she noticed the heavy gold bracelets had gone
her arms became free to fly and hands wave.
She could feel the breeze, she could feel the wind;
it lifted her.
She was too busy meeting, greeting, smiling and asking
that she forgot the web of scars deeply carved
into her body.

The next thing she noticed was the murmuring of her heart.
It started as little escapes of air, puffs and sparks
sometimes it tickled but there was nothing to scratch
and then slowly and slowly new people filled up the spaces.
Her heavy heart was now light, fluffy and
very open
a blossoming red rose.

Had there been a metal, corroded brace strapped tightly to her head
holding in the rage,
a furious fire wanting to explode?
Did she hold the key to the door of her wounds crisscrossed on her being?
Would the diamond encrusted key shine like a rainbow
magically calling up the new cells that would lift
the old into amethyst drops?
And that was when it happened, although she knew not the exact moment.
The head brace had dissolved, her body glowed with
skin anew
and the shedded skin lay on the bathroom floor, dead and diseased.
So she wrapped it up carefully, folding each delicate fragile piece
and into an envelope it went, sealed and scribbled in capitals the solitary word
SURVIVED.

HIGHLY COMMENDED

Labelled

Noeleen Smullen
Ireland

The first time I heard it,
I thought they said crooner.
And I adjusted the hearing aid,
And I thought
Sure I can't sing.
Silly Me.
No.
Cocooner.
Mask me up. Sanitise me up. Lock me up.
Where are my family, my friends, my foes?
Where are my familiar faces?
Some are dead now.
Don't touch him.
Don't touch her.
Don't touch them.
Don't touch.
Wave to me from afar. I'm over here.
No.
Stay away. Keep back.
Further back.
Radio talk shows.
Discussions, dissections. deliberations, dedications.
Countrymen supporting me from afar.
Stay firm. Stay strong. Stay sane.
I'm trying.
Where's my fresh air, my social evenings,
my seventy years of normal?
I want them back.
The laughter, the jokes, the arguments.
I miss them.
And they miss me.
They've taken away the label now.
And yet,
I'm still afraid.

Sunday Papers
Ted Stanley
United Kingdom

I am not the romantic novel you curl up with on a winters evening by a roaring fire.

I am not the inspirational biography that speaks of courage, fortitude and love.

I am not a guide to self-improvement, your road map to a perfect life.

I am not predictable or certain, not safe nor sure.

I am not the happy ending that you seek

I am the Sunday papers that clatter uninvited though your letterbox
Landing with a dream shattering thud on your welcome mat

I am the Sunday papers full of social gossip
Cryptic crosswords, strip cartons and horoscopes.

I am the Sunday papers with exotic recipes
That you cut out to share with other friends on other days
But now forgotten, gathering dust in kitchen drawers
Until discovered sometime later, fading print and curling edges
And you wonder why and where and when and…who?

I am the Sunday papers, now discarded
Strewn across your still warm rumpled bed
While you pursue the romantic dream
That has captured your heart, defined your life
Foretold the happy ending that you seek

SHORTLISTED

Back to the Sea
Anne Steward
United Kingdom

How wrong it feels that we sit, lie, stand
facing into the land, with our backs to the sea.
We, long-primed to search horizons,
and yet, here we are, our red-rimmed eyes
watch trees dance in flame-swept dervish
against orange skies, the song of surf lost to
roars of flames sweeping away
what we thought we knew would last forever.
And we come to where our story began,
to stare towards what it has become.

Yet there it is.
The sea will rise.
As ice melts and slips away
from land after polar land
then we must be aware
of change to come,
and watch for tides
that can swamp our lives.
We will swing like a vane
from threat to threat,
holding tight to small hands
of those who have earned none of this.

SECOND PLACE

Remembrance Day
Tim Taylor
United Kingdom

Once more, they come
from their forgotten places
unearthed and put on show like relics,
caps and blazers brand them
as belonging in another time.

Pipes and drumbeats
pump new vigour into creaking limbs
a bugler summons up the dead
to be remembered. Old men weep
and feel ashamed to have survived.

November hurls its tears into their faces
bouquets of leaves around their feet
and blows a wild Last Post
as cars and coaches suck them back
into invisibility.

It matters to them
to have done their duty by their pals
but there's another reason why they came:
to count for something, even for a day,
to march, just one more time
into the light.

Highly Commended

West Shore
Tim Taylor
United Kingdom

This place possessed you:
the essence of it, borne on sea spray
sank into your bones.
Fleeting light on soft grey waves,
their lilting sussurations
flowed through eyes and ears
to sow a seed of it in you
that took root and grew
like sea grass, swaying
in the tides of life
but tenacious, holding on
to bring you back, and back again.

It was two-way osmosis:
pervading everything, this shore
in turn was steeped in you.
Elsewhere, you left a vacuum,
nothing but aching emptiness,
but here, replanting
ancient footsteps, I sense you still
within the glint of sun on water
the salt taste in the air
and the soothing surf
that reassures me
'sshhh, I am at peace.'

SHORTLISTED

More than alive;
Dawn Vincent
United Kingdom

I want punctuation beyond
the hopeful semi-colon;
I want everything but full stops.
I want exclamations and questions,
dashes and commas
and some days nothing but breathless words.

I don't just want ellipses suggesting
there will be more to come.
I need it all now – this beautiful, vital life.
I need more than survival – more than
just bones needing blood,
I want to thrive on the marrow of everything.

Birthday Cake
Matt Wixey
United Kingdom

We let so few people within the reach of our arms;
Our spheres have tightened, and shrunk.
Pupils contracting against a glaring and terrible sun.
It is necessary
To protect ourselves.
Like wagons ringed we bristle outwards,
And in this way cannot be hurt.

Wise words from my mother,
A birthday gift for a scared and lonely child:
Never trust people.
People will break your heart.

Vast walls built with that gift, still stand,
Each event another stratum to hold them fast
Against the sea.
Scarred from ancient attempts
To scale them or break them down.
Algae feeds and thrives in the cracks.

I want the walls to decay more, each year,
Become pointless with the changing of borders,
And the unseen shifting of plates deep beneath us.
Like when we wish each other *happy birthday.*

Where once I heard a tired and well-worn phrase,
Now a controlled demolition
In the blast of the words unsaid:
I am glad you came into the world and
I am glad you are alive.
There is no armour, against weapons like that.

Each time I blow out lit candles,
I make a wish to be defenceless again.

SHORTLISTED

Choices
Valerie Wynne
United Kingdom

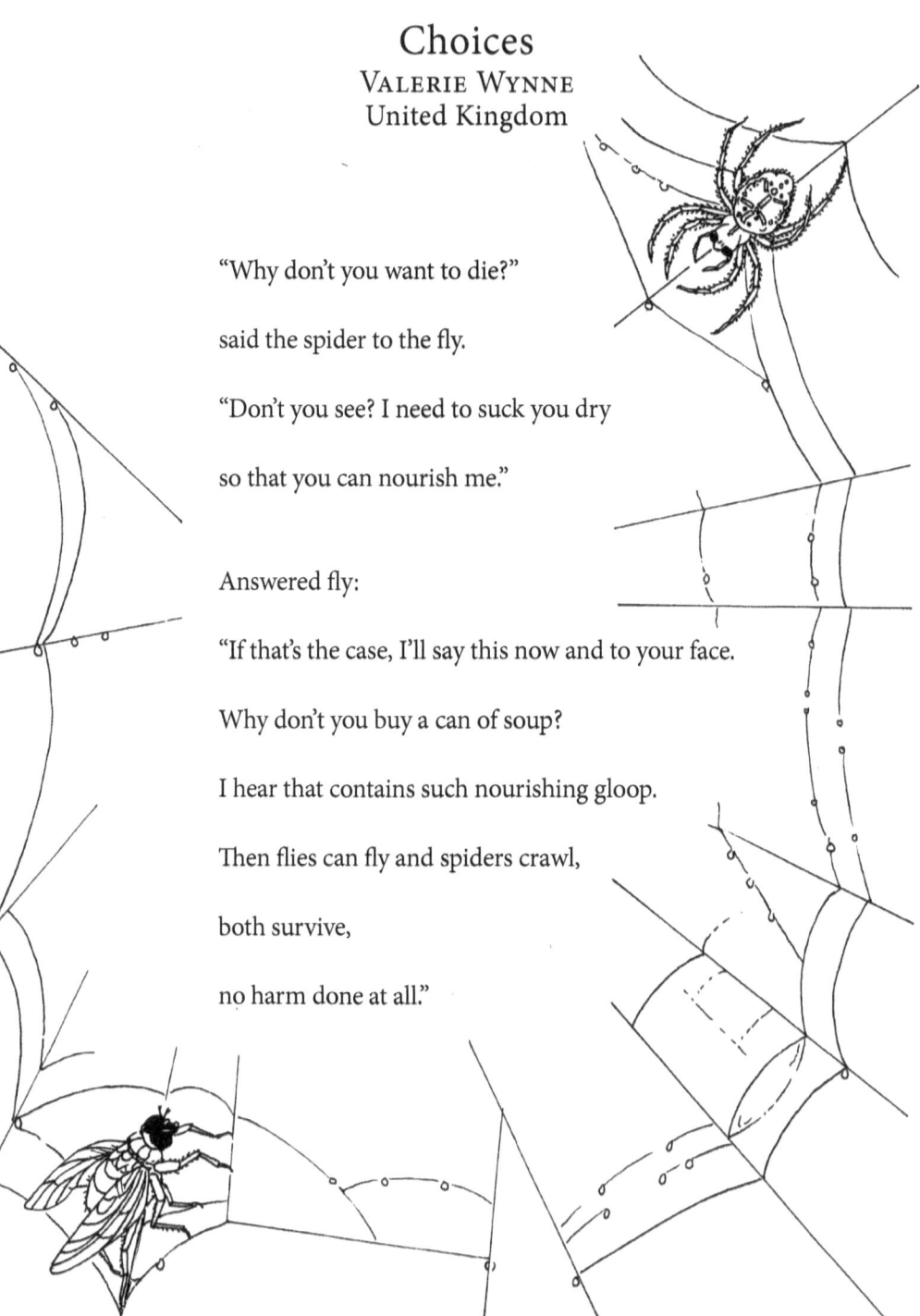

"Why don't you want to die?"

said the spider to the fly.

"Don't you see? I need to suck you dry

so that you can nourish me."

Answered fly:

"If that's the case, I'll say this now and to your face.

Why don't you buy a can of soup?

I hear that contains such nourishing gloop.

Then flies can fly and spiders crawl,

both survive,

no harm done at all."

SHORTLISTED

Survival, But
Kathy Zwick
United Kingdom

Elizabeth, just 13, cries through long good-byes.
She will never see her four older siblings, never, ever again.
She sets off for lands unknown.

Elizabeth survived the trip. Shyly, she admired from afar
a hale young indentured servant lad, who tumbled overboard,
a lusty lad, more an adventurer than a saint. Loyal fast-thinking
nimble mates hurled down a long hemp halyard and hauled him up,
up from the greedy, grasping, encroaching icy waves.
Miraculously, he survived.

But, two parents, aunt and uncle died. Again she cried.
Cruel winter's tear-eyed orphan, just 14, kindly taken in
by Governor John Carver, his wife, and three lodgers.

Autumn harvest, Elizabeth – one of just 22 surviving,
resilient children. For their chores - many tasks:
To welcome kindly, to say thank you to the generous menu-mentors,
neighbours (90!), friendly members of the Wampanoag tribe.
She serves adult hosts and guests at a sumptuous three-day feast,
eating, singling, dancing, and feisty games. Kids ate last.
What would she wear? Well, nothing new this year.
An old, once brightly coloured, adult-like longish dress,
sparse cargo packed, way back - a hard, long, long year ago.

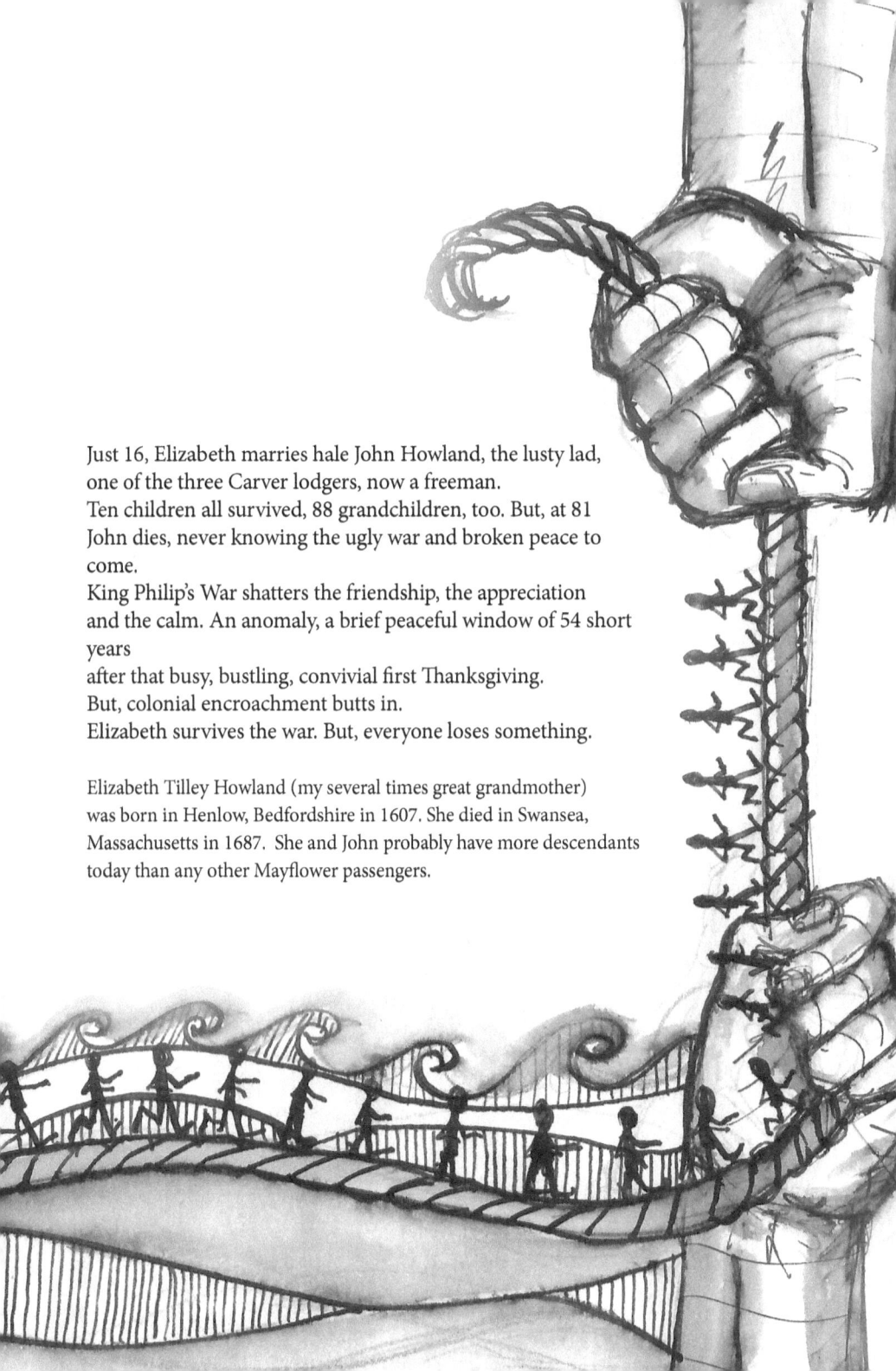

Just 16, Elizabeth marries hale John Howland, the lusty lad,
one of the three Carver lodgers, now a freeman.
Ten children all survived, 88 grandchildren, too. But, at 81
John dies, never knowing the ugly war and broken peace to
come.
King Philip's War shatters the friendship, the appreciation
and the calm. An anomaly, a brief peaceful window of 54 short
years
after that busy, bustling, convivial first Thanksgiving.
But, colonial encroachment butts in.
Elizabeth survives the war. But, everyone loses something.

Elizabeth Tilley Howland (my several times great grandmother)
was born in Henlow, Bedfordshire in 1607. She died in Swansea,
Massachusetts in 1687. She and John probably have more descendants
today than any other Mayflower passengers.

Hammond House is a social enterprise membership organisation founded by students at the *University Centre Grimsby* and run by volunteers. We aim to encourage and support creative talent in art and literature, providing opportunities for members to showcase their work and develop a succesful career.

Our current activities include publishing, literary competitions, filmmaking, TV productions, writing workshops, festival and community engagement programmes.

Members benefit from reduced competition fees, and opportunities to showcase their work or get involved in our wide range of creative activities.

We are planning to offer a range of publishing options to new writers, and expand our programme to engage with isolated people in both rural and urban communities through art and literature.

www.hammondhousepublishing.com

2020 International Literary Prize

The fifth year of this prestigious literary prize saw a record number of entries spread across five continents.

1st Place	Walkabout	Jean Cooper Moran
2nd Place	Remembrance Day	Tim Taylor
3rd Place	Dirt	Mason Nunemaker

Three entries were Highly Commended, eighteen entries were shortlisted, two were added as Judges Choices, and three were included as Editor's Choice.

The competition judges this year were:
Steve Jackson, William Hatchett and Paul Sutherland.

Awarded by the *University Centre Grimsby*

www.hammondhousepublishing.com

2021 International Literary Prize

Awarded by the University Centre Grimsby, winners receive a cash prize, and worldwide publication of their work in an anthology, together with shortlisted entries.

1st Prize	£500
2nd Prize	£100
3rd Prize	£50

Worldwide publication for the shortlisted stories

Theme: STARDUST
1 Poem
Entries open from 26th February 2020
Submission deadline: 30th September 2020

OTHER 2020 COMPETITIONS:
International Short Story Prize
International Screenplay Prize
International Songwriting Prize

www.hammondhousepublishing.com

HAMMOND HOUSE PRODUCTIONS

Hammond House Productions is a Grimsby-based media company that tells compelling stories through corporate videos, documentaries, promotional videos and TV programmes.

We help forward thinking organisations respond to the challenges and opportunities provided by search engines, social media, local and regional television channels, and digital communications.

As part of the Hammond House group we support and encourage the development of creative talent.

www.hammondhouseproductions.com

BillboardTV

Billboard is a monthly programme produced by members of the Hammond House group, covering theatre, music, art and literature in East Yorkshire and Lincolnshire, going behind the scenes of your favourite shows, reviewing the latest film releases, books and art exhibitions. interviewing local celebrities and showcasing local musicians.

Billboard provides a great opportunity to showcase member's skills and pursue the Hammond House mission to encourage local talent and engage with the local people.

www.billboardtv.uk

CleeTV

The traditional English seaside town of Cleethorpes was first established in the 6th century as a fishing village and developed into a popular holiday resort in the 19th Century.

Clee TV provides a range of programmes for locals and vistors that celebrate its heritage and covers news, local events, entertainment, and local music.

www.clee.tv

HH | HAMMOND HOUSE GALLERY

Part of the Hammond House social enterprise, the gallery exhibits original artwork by local artists, hosts talks on buying and collecting art, holds art workshops and sponsors open art competitions.

www.hammondhousegallery.com

HAMMOND HOUSE WRITERS

A place where writers of all ages, disciplines and standards can develop their talent, connect with other writers, enjoy exclusive competitions and even get published. Sponsored by the University Centre Grimsby and funded by the National Lottery.

WRITERS GROUPS
Joining a writer's group gives you the opportunity to make new friends, exchange ideas and get feedback on your work from others who share your passion. Our help and support is now available to both established groups, and new groups starting out.

ACADEMY
Our video workshops can help to brush up your creative writing skills. Developing your ability to communicate ideas in an effective and interesting way offers many social and professional advantages.

WELLBEING
Our wellbeing workshops help you to use writing to stay healthy and beat loneliness, depression and other mental health issues.

www.hammondhousewriters.com

The University Centre Grimsby, as part
of the Grimsby Institute, is built on
high expectations, a focus on learning,
commitment to achievement and an engaged,
practical education for all students.

A wide range of degree level courses are
available including BA (hons) Creative and
Professional Writing.

www.grimsby.ac.uk

www.ingramcontent.com/pod-product-compliance
Lightning Source LLC
Chambersburg PA
CBHW030308100526
44590CB00012B/564